DANGEROUS WORK!

LUMBERJACK

THEIA LAKE

PowerKiDS press

Published in 2026 by The Rosen Publishing Group, Inc.
2544 Clinton Street, Buffalo, NY 14224

First Edition

Editor: Greg Roza
Book Design: Rachel Rising

Photo Credits: Cover, Peter Kniez/Shutterstock.com; Cover, pp. 1, 3-24 Pattern image/Shutterstock.com; p. 4 Cherdchai101/Shutterstock.com; p. 5 tetxu/Shutterstock.com; p. 6 on and Joe/Shutterstock.com; p.7 https://commons.wikimedia.org/wiki/File:Logging_Scene_Near_Bellingham,_WA.jpg; pp. 8, 11 Kletr/Shutterstock.com; p. 9 Robert Schneider/Shutterstock.com;p.10 Amy Johansson/Shutterstock.com; p. 12 Anterovium/Shutterstock.com; p. 13 Inna G/Shutterstock.com; p. 15 Juriah Mosin/Shutterstock.com; p. 16 Random435/Shutterstock.com; p. 17 tetxu/Shutterstock.com; p. 18 Pixel-Shot/Shutterstock.com; p.19 Mark Agnor/Shutterstock.com;p. 21 meunierd/Shutterstock.com.

Library of Congress Cataloging-in-Publication Data

Names: Lake, Theia, author.
Title: Lumberjack / Theia Lake.
Description: [Buffalo] : PowerKids Press, [2026] | Series: Dangerous work! | Includes bibliographical references and index.
Identifiers: LCCN 2024060787 (print) | LCCN 2024060788 (ebook) | ISBN 9781499452372 (library binding) | ISBN 9781499452365 (paperback) | ISBN 9781499452389 (ebook)
Subjects: LCSH: Loggers–Juvenile literature. | Logging–Vocational guidance–Juvenile literature.
Classification: LCC SD538 .L35 2026 (print) | LCC SD538 (ebook) | DDC 634.9/8023–dc23/eng/20250213
LC record available at https://lccn.loc.gov/2024060787
LC ebook record available at https://lccn.loc.gov/2024060788

Manufactured in the United States of America

CPSIA Compliance Information: Batch #CSPK26. For Further Information contact Rosen Publishing at 1-800-237-9932.

CONTENTS

TIMBER!

Picture yourself standing on the edge of a thick forest. It's your job to remove large, old trees that may be a danger to campers and hikers. You have climbing tools, a hardhat, and a chainsaw. Time to get to work, lumberjack!

Lumberjacks have long been important to the growth and success of American communities. They clear land and collect trees to create lumber. They are trained to use dangerous power tools and **vehicles**. Read on to find out what it takes to become a lumberjack!

STAY SAFE!

It was once common for lumberjacks to yell out "Timber!" to warn fellow workers of a falling tree.

The word "lumberjack" was first used in Canada in the 1830s. Other words in use at that time include "lumberman" and "timberjack." Today, it's more common to use the word "logger."

A BRIEF HISTORY

Logging began in the United States when the first Europeans settled in the area that became Jamestown, Virgina. They needed to clear the land for homes and farms. They used simple tools, mostly axes and handsaws. As settlers moved west, logging continued to be very important to the growing country.

Early logging often took place in winter, when the ground was hard enough to pull wagons full of freshly cut trees. Early logging camps were incredibly wild and dangerous places.

STAY SAFE!

You might think of the tall tale of Paul Bunyan when you hear the word lumberjack. Bunyan is a **symbol** of the hard work and the brave men of the logging **industry** in the United States.

This postcard from 1910 shows a team of loggers in the State of Washington posing near a huge tree they recently took down.

JOBS IN THE FOREST

There are many jobs out there for trained lumberjacks. They work for construction companies, parks, logging companies, arborists, and more.

Fallers are lumberjacks that cut down trees. But lumberjacks don't just cut down trees. Tree climbers climb tall trees to remove branches and to cut the tops off them. Buckers cut logs into shorter pieces. Graders inspect logs and decide where they will be shipped and how they will be used. Some lumberjacks are trained heavy vehicle drivers.

An arborist is someone trained in the planting, growth, care, and removal of trees. Arborists are sometimes called tree **surgeons**!

LOGGING LOCATIONS

Logging usually takes place in wild locations. The place could be very cold or very hot, but lumberjacks still have a job to do. Lumberjacks don't work in hard rain because that makes the job even more dangerous.

Lumberjacks must be aware of their surroundings at all times. Wooded places can have uneven ground, rivers, cliffs, and even **poisonous** plants and animals. Large trucks are needed to move fallen trees. Large cranes are used to load the trucks. These vehicles can be dangerous to work on and around.

This logging vehicle has a crane to grab logs and a place to stack them for **transportation**. It also has special tires for moving over uneven ground.

TOOLS OF THE TRADE

Lumberjacks have long used simple axes and handsaws, and they still do! However, modern loggers use power tools as well. The most common power tool is the chainsaw. This tool has a circular chain with sharp metal teeth on it. The chain spins very quickly and cuts through wood.

Tree climbers are trained to climb high into the air with a chainsaw on the end of a rope! Once they are in position, they start the saw and lop off branches or the top of the tree itself.

Lumberjacks need to stay safe. They wear glasses, hardhats, and heavy gloves. They also wear ear plugs to keep their ears safe.

LUMBERJACK SKILLS

Lumberjacks need to be strong and fit. They spend a lot of time lifting heavy machines, controlling buzzing chainsaws, and moving giant logs. Lumberjacks should also enjoy working outside, even in bad weather.

Taking care of logging tools is important. A dull chainsaw won't cut as well, and can lead to **accidents**. Lumberjacks know how to sharpen chainsaws and axes. Many know how to use a **compass**. Other important skills include knowledge of poisonous plants and animals, putting out fires, and planting new trees.

STAY SAFE!

A full-grown tree can weigh 5 tons (4.5 mt) or more. It's very important for loggers to pay attention to the work they and others are doing so they don't get crushed by a falling tree . . . timber!

Some lumberjacks are so good with a chainsaw they can use one to make sculptures out of wood or ice!

TRAINING AND EDUCATION

Logging companies usually want workers with a high school education. Classes you may want to take include woodworking and environmental science. Weight training classes will help you get in shape!

Many logging companies offer on-the-job training. However, you can also take a **forestry** course. You will learn how to **survey** forests, identify different kinds of trees and plants, and make guesses on the value of wood. Some forestry programs offer certifications in logging. Certifications are official papers that show future employers you are well trained.

Safety is another topic all loggers need training in. It's important to know how to react when an accident happens.

GET A JOB!

The first step when looking for a logging job is to research logging companies near where you live. Some states have more forests, and therefore they offer more logging jobs. Some people decide to move closer to those jobs.

To start, you might work as an apprentice. That means you learn from trained loggers. You might need to do jobs others don't want to do. However, you can move up after proving yourself as a strong worker.

Keep in mind that some logging jobs are seasonal. Others are limited or part-time job offers.

THE RIGHT JOB FOR YOU?

Today, logging workers are paid between $30,000 and $70,000, depending on the job and level of training. Loggers may also have to drive farther to get to work, and may need to buy costly tools. Working for a logging company can be dangerous but if you remember your training and follow safety rules, logging can be a great job for young workers.

If you are looking for an exciting job that keeps you fit as you work outside, lumberjack might be the perfect one for you!

STAY SAFE!

Log rolling events come from the fact that loggers used to float logs down rivers to saw mills. Skilled lumberjacks rode the logs and used long poles to keep them from getting jammed up.

Lumberjack competitions, or events, honor old logging practices. These include sawing races, tree climbing races, and log rolling!

GLOSSARY

accident: An unintended and usually sudden event resulting in loss or hurt.

compass: A tool the shows direction by means of a magnetic needle pointing to the magnetic north.

forestry: The science and practice of caring for forests.

industry: A group of businesses that provide a certain product or service.

poisonous: Having poison, or a substance that can cause illness or death when touched or taken into the body.

surgeon: A trained doctor who cuts into the body to heal it.

survey: To measure and examine an area of land.

symbol: Something that stands for something else.

transportation: The act of moving people or objects from one place to another.

vehicle: A machine used to carry things from one place to another.

FOR MORE INFORMATION

BOOKS

Apps-Bodily, Susan, and Jerry Apps. *Timber! A Northwoods Story of Lumberjacks, Logging, and the Land.* Madison, WI: Wisconsin Historical Society Press, 2024.

Hudak, Heather C. *Paul Bunyan and Babe the Blue Ox.* Minneapolis MN: Abdo, 2023.

WEBSITES

Logging Facts for Kids
kids.kiddle.co/Logging
Read much more about the U.S. logging industry and see amazing historical photographs.

Lumberjack World Championships
lumberjackworldchampionships.com
Check out the exciting events at the Lumberjack World Championship held every year in Hayward, Wisconsin.

INDEX